This book is dedicated to all Historians!

*Thank you for caring enough to want to learn more.
Thank you for not allowing our past to be forgotten.*

In Memory of Kathryn Coombs (1953-2011)

The Way They Were: Dressed in 1860-1865

A Photographic Reference
Volume 2

By Donna J. Abraham

Copyright © 2011 Donna J. Abraham

Published on behalf of Abraham's Lady, LLC.

Written and produced by Abraham's Lady, LLC.

All of the carte de visite images are the property of Donna Abraham and Abraham's Lady, LLC.

Printed and bound in the United States of America.

All rights reserved. No part of this book may be used or reproduced without written permission of the author except in the case of brief quotations embodied in critical essays and reviews.

ISBN-978-1-57747-156-1

Contents

Note from the Author 6

Introduction 7

1. Fashions for Women
   Dress Fabrics 10
      Plaids • Stripes • Squares • Prints
   Special Dresses 18
      Mourning • Sheer • Fancy
   Dress Trims 23
   Hairstyles 31
   Hair Covers 36
   Caps 40
   Accessories 42
      Undersleeves • Fans • Neck bows • Jewelry •
      Aprons • Handkerchiefs • Collars and Cuffs •
      Mitts • Belts • Pockets • Baskets •
      Shawls • Jackets
   Outer Wear 70
      Hats • Bonnets • Gloves • Cloaks and Capes •
      Coats • Furs

2. Fashions for Children
   Infants 81
   Girls 85
      Toddlers • Young Girls • Adolescents • Teenagers
   Boys 103
      Toddlers • Young Boys • Adolescents • Teenagers

3. Fashions for Men
   Hair and Hats 112
   Neckwear and Vests 117
   Coats and Trousers 125

4. Family and Friends 128

Additional Reading 143

About the Author 144

A Note From The Author

I am often asked what led me to become an author of non-fiction history reference books. My answer to that question is that it was the series of positive life choices listed below that somehow all added up to equal this remarkable result.

A love of history +
A passion for exploring antique stores and flea markets +
A college degree in Home Economics +
Specializations in tailoring, pattern drafting, clothing construction +
A college degree in Elementary Education +
Teaching reading +
Teaching History of Fashion and Clothing Construction +
Civil War Reenacting +
A Carte De Viste collection of over one thousand photos +
A large collection of original 1860s clothing and accessories +
Research on the clothes worn by Americans from 1860-1865 +
Building a business dedicated to authentic clothing reproducions +
A desire to share my research, collections, and knowledge =

My first book – *The Way They Were: Dressed In 1860-1865* +
Huge success of the book =

My second book – *The Way They Were: Dressed In 1860-1865, Volume 2*

Introduction

A new photographic process that was developed in the late 1850s produced photos that were later called Cartes De Viste or CDV's. These photos made it possible for much of the population to have a "likeness" of themselves or loved ones. The CDV was known as the "Poor Man's Portrait" because they were inexpensive and multiple copies were available. The peak years of popularity for this format were 1859-1866. The images in this book are all Cartes De Viste that have been carefully selected to make sure that they are specifically from 1860-1865.

As you view these images please keep in mind that the individuals in the photos are real Americans. People of the 1860s were like us in many respects: some were very fashionable, some were not, some were photogenic, and some were not. They came from all walks of life, various economic classes and different geographic regions.

Since this photo process was so new, people did not smile while having their photo taken because they were trying to look dignified in the same manner as sitting for an oil portrait. Individuals wore their best clothes for the procedure. The chemicals used to develop the photos caused colors of the clothing and accessories to appear very different in the Carte De Viste than in real life; for example, light blue and yellow could look black in a CDV.

Each Carte De Viste has so much to tell us! All of the images in this book have been magnified so the clothing and accessory details can be easily examined. The photos are placed into chapters that best illustrate that topic. Each chapter contains different age groups and various designs to provide a good selection of examples.

This book is a marvelous compilation of American women, children and men, *The Way They Were: Dressed In 1860-1865, Volume 2.*

This stunning collection provides visual inspiration and will serve as an authentic reference guide to the reader.

Enjoy!

Donna Abraham
Gettysburg, PA

Acknowledgments

A loving thank you to my husband, Bob Abraham.

A huge thank you to four awesome ladies: Beth Atkins, Denise Moriarty, Trudy Nelson and Kathy Starkweather. They expertly ran my business, Abraham's Lady in Gettysburg, PA while I was away writing this book.

Special thanks to Jim Thomas of Thomas Publications, Gettysburg, PA for making my book look magnificent!

1
Fashions for Women

**Dress Fabrics • Special Dresses • Dress Trims
Hairstyles • Hair Covers • Accessories
Wraps • Outer Wear**

Dress Fabrics

Plaids • Stripes • Squares • Prints

Even though the fitted bodice, full skirt dress styles did not vary greatly, the dress appearance was changed by the use of various fabric types, designs and trims.

Wool, silk, cotton, or blends of wool and silk were the fabric choices for making dresses.

Fabrics that had woven or printed designs on them were commonly used to make dresses during this time period. They were well liked because the prints were less likely to show stains and fading. An array of fabric colors were available, with most being similar to colors found in nature. Fabric prints, plaids, and squares varied in size and often, when the dress pieces were sewn together, these designs were not carefully matched in order to save fabric. Dots and clusters of objects such as flowers were often used in prints in large and small scale.

Dress fabrics – Plaids

Dress fabrics – Stripes

Dress fabrics – Squares

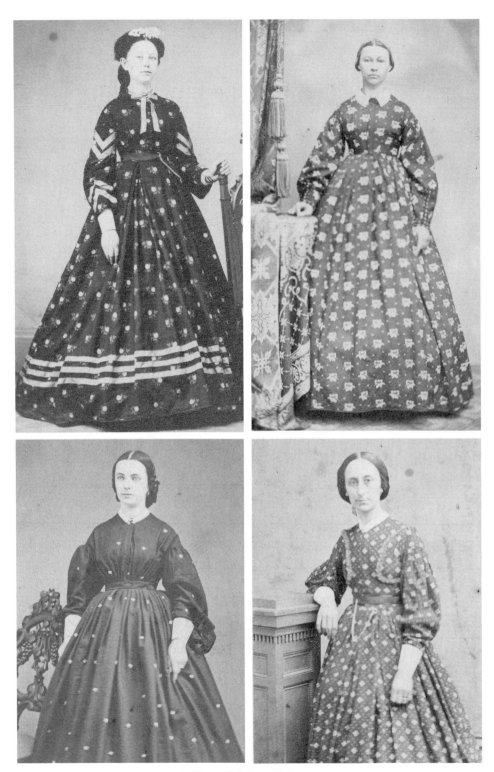

Dress fabrics – Prints

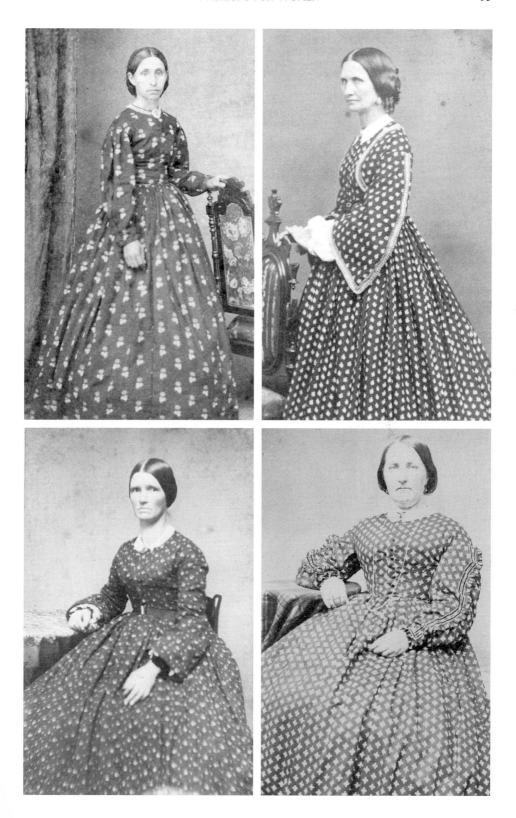

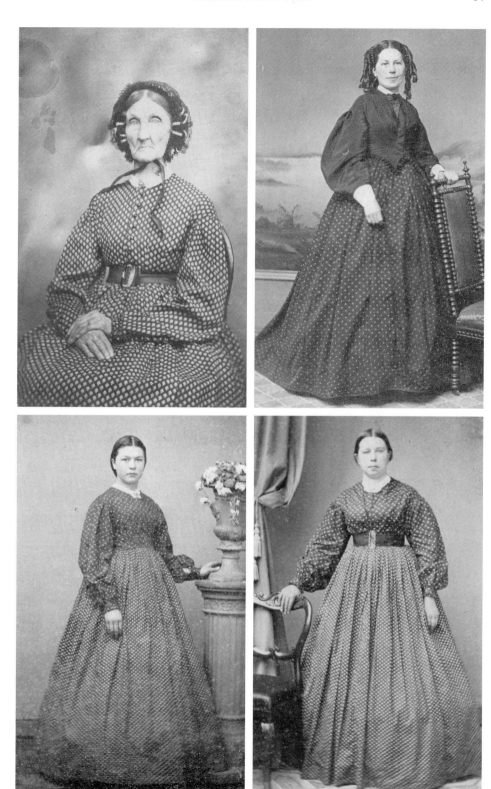

Special Dresses

MOURNING • SHEER • FANCY

Mourning dresses — The typical lady in the early stages of mourning who appeared in public would be wearing all black attire. The mourning bonnet and dress were made of dull black fabric and trimmed in crape. The veil was silk and its density and size depended on the stage of mourning. Gloves were usually black in color, although white gloves were also considered appropriate.

Crape was a crimped dull black silk fabric that was used in the 19th century to show that the wearer was in mourning. It was used as a trim on clothing, bonnets, and veils. The amount of crape added to a garment depended on the period of mourning the person was in with the most crape usage to signify the deepest mourning stage.

Sheer Dresses — *Sheer fabric dresses were worn in the hot weather. The lady was still covered neck to toe, but the thinness of the fabric allowed air to reach the arms and shoulder area for some welcome relief from the heat.*

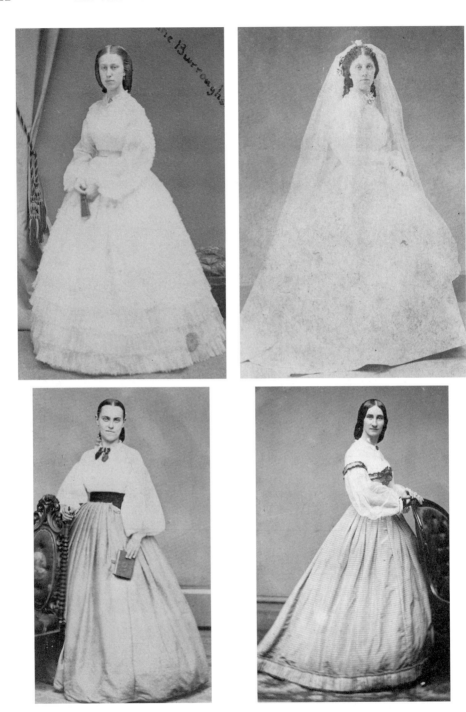

Fancy Dresses — Fancy day dresses were often made of silk with an abundance of ruffles and flounces. This extravagant use of fabric was reserved for upper class ladies. Wedding dresses were usually a lady's best dress. The use of the white wedding dress with a long veil was just becoming popular in the 1860s. The light colored Garibaldi blouse with its voluminous sleeves and skirt was a new style and was considered very fancy.

Dress Trims

Decorative trim made of wool, silk, or cotton was used to individualize a lady's dress. It was used mainly in rows around the skirt bottom, on the bodice near the shoulders, and on the sleeves. Bands of fabric, ribbons, and braid were sewn in geometric designs or rows. Ruffles, pleats and ruching were less common trims for dresses due to their high cost. Although most trims were a variety of colors, lace was only available in black, white, and off-white. Buttons were added as decorations and were often placed over the bodice hook and eye closure. All trims were positioned on the dresses to make the waistline appear small and the rest of the body look wide.

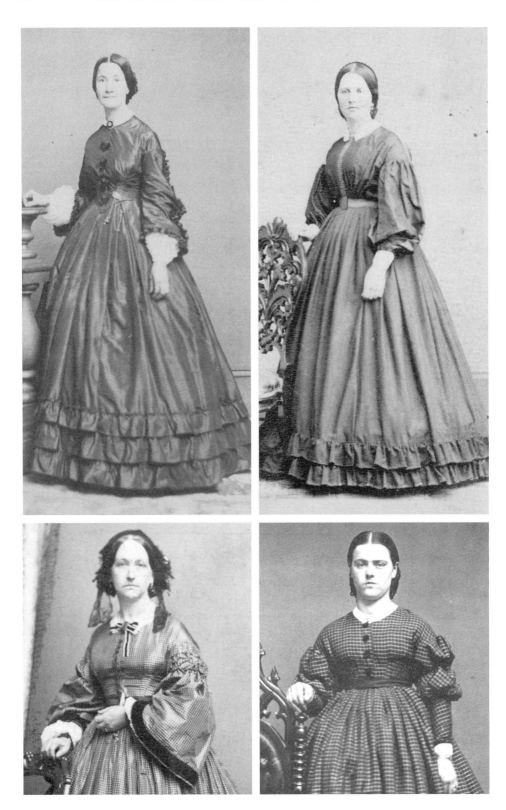

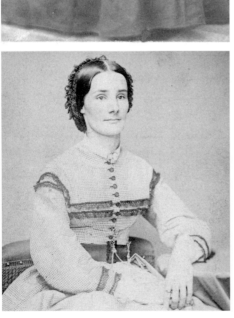

Hairstyles

Most ladies in the 1860-1865 time period wore their hair confined with few variations. Hair was usually parted in the center of the head and flattened on the crown with no bangs which created an illusion of height. The hair on the side of the head was arranged by twisting or braiding, and secured to the back of the head with a few ringlets or by simply smoothing it over or behind the ears. The hair in back was confined; often pulled together at the base of the head in an arrangement of ringlets, buns, rolls, or chignons. Hair fillers (a person's hair saved from hairbrushes), hair pieces, and braids were used to enhance the hairstyle. Short and unrestrained hair was not a popular style of the period.

Hair Covers

The fine hair net was used to cover the lady's hair. It was made of silk or real hair and was close to the actual hair color because it was used to keep the hair in place, not to act as an adornment. Another style of hair net that was used as a decoration over the hair was woven using thicker yarn or ribbons. It could be a different color than the hair and some were ornamented with beads. Another favorite hair cover was the banded hair net. These were constructed of braided or pleated ribbon or lace and occasionally had tassels or long ribbons hanging on the sides.

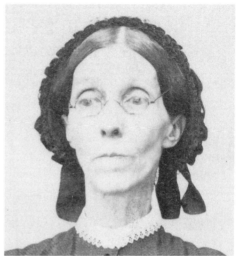

Caps

Caps were worn as an indoor head cover. Different caps were worn at different times of the day, but all were made of delicate fabric trimmed with lace, ribbon, and sometimes had long ties or lappets draped on each side of the head. The cap was positioned on the top of the head and hung down the back to cover and confine the hair.

Accessories

UNDERSLEEVES • FANS • NECK BOWS • JEWELRY
HANDKERCHIEFS • APRONS • COLLARS AND CUFFS • MITTS • BELTS
POCKETS • BASKETS • SHAWLS • JACKETS

The following pages in this section illustrate the many items used to accessorize a woman's appearance.

Undersleeves — partial sleeves worn under the loose sleeve of the bodice to prevent the wrists and forearm from showing. They were commonly white and made of delicate fabrics and sometimes trimmed with lace.

Fans — *Hand-held folding fans were constructed of wood, tortoise shell or ivory slats and covered with stiff pleated cotton, paper or silk. They were made to be either half-round or full-round when opened.*

A plain, non-folding style of fan made of woven palmetto leaves was also available and was used by men and women.

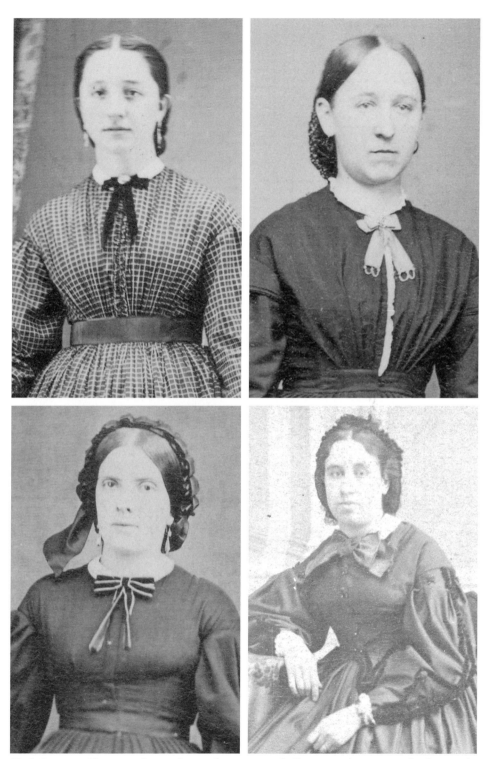

Neck Bows — Very popular and worn by women of all ages and economic backgrounds. They were attached to the neckline of the bodice by pins or simply tied around the neck.

 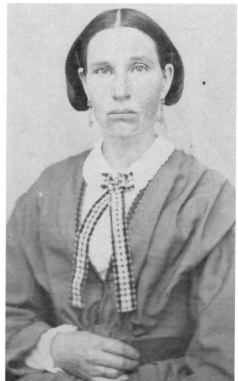

Jewelry — Brooches, earrings, bracelets, and watch chains were common accessories.

    Brooches were worn at the center front of the bodice neckline. They were usually made of gold or pinchback (an imitation of gold) and often held a loved one's image or lock of hair. Other popular brooch forms depicted classical or biblical scenes on carved shell or lava rock. Gem stones and colored glass was also used. Gutta purcha, bog oak, and jet brooches often featured intricate designs and could also be worn as mourning jewelry due the to dark color.

    Earrings were available in many patterns including hoops. They were all made for pierced ears and utilized curved hooks.

    Bracelets were chunky in size and often worn in pairs, one on each wrist. Earrings and bracelets were made from the same materials as brooches.

    Long pocket watch chains were attached to the bodice hook or a button with the watch tucked behind a belt or held in a small pocket.

Aprons — Special aprons made of fine cotton, silk, or wool were used as a dress accessory rather than dress protection. Therefore, they did not have a "bib" that covered the dress bodice. This fancy item often featured intricately sewn trims and embroidered designs.

Handkerchiefs — Lady's handkerchiefs were large, solid squares made of white linen or fine cotton bordered with deep, rich lace. Handkerchiefs used during the mourning period were still white cotton, but edged in black.

Collars — Every day dress had a one-piece collar of some kind. The collars were white or a light color and made of a fine solid cotton fabric, plain, or edged with trim. This curved collar varied in width from about one and one-half to two inches. Collars made entirely of lace were sometimes used on fancy day dresses. The collar was made as a separate piece from the dress and bodice. Evidence shows that they were sometimes held at the neckline with a brooch or pins rather than sewn on.

Cuffs sewn onto a dress bodice were an interesting design feature. They were often the same fabric as the bodice with the addition of trim, lace, ruching, or ruffles. Easy to clean, detachable cuffs were made in all widths. The cuff fabric usually matched the collar.

Mitts — Made of fine silk or cotton lace, mitts were wrist high. Available in two styles, either a half-finger length or those that just covered the palm/back of the hand. Most often worn by older women, however all ages were photographed wearing them.

Belts — *The belt was a common accessory that was worn by women of all ages. It came in widths from one and one-half to four inches and was made of grosgrain ribbon, stiff fabric, or thin leather. The buckle used with the belt was generally taller than its width and matched the width of the belt. The styles of buckle available were a two-piece center hook type, a simple one-piece slide through, or a three to four prong design. Belt pins came in various lengths and were used to fasten the belt overlap.*

Pockets — Pockets on the outside of the dress were usually small and seemed to be more decorative than functional. If a pocket was attached near the waist, it was often used to hold a watch.

Baskets — The lidded basket seemed to be a popular carry-all of the 1860s. They were woven and made of thin wooden slats or reeds. They had a matching lid and stiff bent handles. Left with a natural finish, they were seldom painted.

Shawls — The shawl was the perfect cool weather wrap to wear with a day dress; keeping the chill off the shoulders it also added beauty to the lady's image. Shawls were large squares of at least sixty inches that were folded and worn as a triangle with the point draped on the back of the skirt. Some were up to three times longer than their width so that they could be folded several times for added warmth.

The Chantilly lace silk shawl was the most intricate with floral motifs woven into the netting. Paisley shawls were made of brightly colored wool yarn in a paisley pattern. Basic wool shawls could also have striped and plaid designs in an array of colors woven around the edges. Fringe trimmed shawls were made in both silk and wool.

The wool knitted or crocheted shawl had light colors accented with bright colored stripes or edges.

Jackets — Worn over day dresses as an outer garment. Popular with all age groups, jacket styles were shorter in length than coats. The body of a jacket was a solid color, but often embellished with trim or fringe around the edges. Occassionally used as part of an ensemble such as with the Garibaldi blouse and shirt.

Outer Wear

HATS • BONNETS • GLOVES • CLOAKS AND CAPES • COATS • FURS

FASHIONS FOR WOMEN

Hats — Flat crowned, wide brimmed hats were worn out of doors and considered country wear. They were often made of woven straw or a stiff form covered with fabric. Feathers, flowers, and ribbons were common embellishments. Long ribbon ties were occassionally used to secure the hat to the head. Hats were worn at the top, center of the head and was not tilted to either side.

Bonnets — The bonnet was an important part of characterizing a lady's appearance; therefore bonnets were very common. They were various shapes, made of plain and figured silk, fine wool, or cotton formed on a stiff foundation. The fabric color did not have to match the dress fabric. Woven straw bonnets were also worn during warm weather. The bonnets were trimmed with artificial flowers, lace, and berries under the top of the brim. The bonnet was secured to the head with a wide ribbon tied in a large bow directly under the chin.

Gloves — Full-fingered kid leather gloves were the most popular and availble in a wide array of colors. Solid cotton fabric full-fingered gloves were a second favorite chioce. White gloves in either leather or cotton were a "must" for evening and formal wear. All glove styles did not extend beyond the wrist.

Capes and Cloaks — Capes and cloaks draped over the lady's full dress and were hemmed to fall twelve to eighteen inches above the bottom of the dress. Most of these cold weather garments were made of wool due to its natural warmth and water repellency. Hoods and arm slits were common variations. Buttons, clasps, hooks and eyes, as well as braided knots and loops were used to keep capes and cloaks closed.

Coats — Lady's who wore coats enjoyed much greater freedom of movement because the coat offered a full sleeve that would easily fit over any bodice sleeve. Otherwise, the characteristics were similar to those of capes and cloaks.

Furs — The fur cuff, collar, mantle, or short cape offered additional warmth to traditional outer wear. The barrel shaped, smooth fur muff kept the hands warm. Decorative tassels added elegance to fur pieces.

2
Fashions for Children

INFANTS • GIRLS • BOYS

Infants

Both male and female infants were dressed in long, white gowns that had wide necklines, short sleeves and full skirts. The gowns were fastened in the back with ties or tiny buttons. Drawstrings at the neck and waist allowed for growth adjustment. The gowns often had decorative stitching or rows of tucks, but seldom had contrasting trim probably because the trim would not withstand frequent laundering.

Hemlines became shorter as the child became more active, but the styles still remained the same for both sexes. The only difference being that boy's dresses had lot of military style trims and braids whereas girl's had delicate prints and lighter colors. As the child aged, their clothing style became more like adult attire.

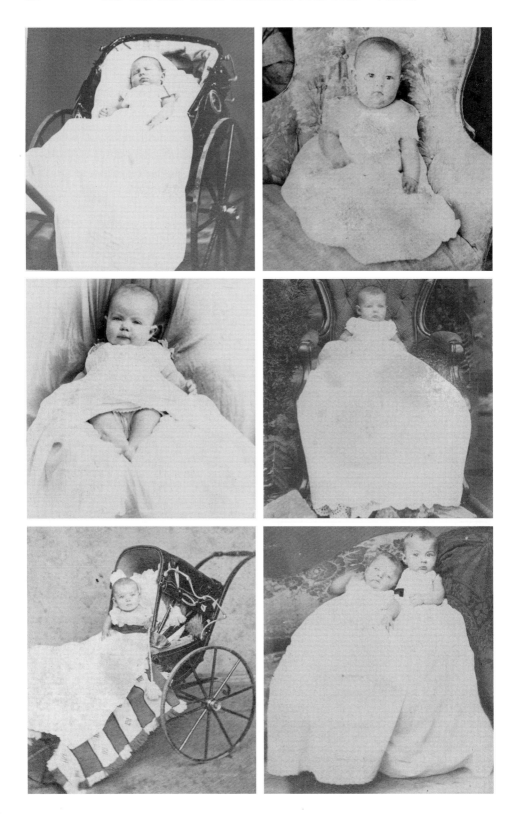

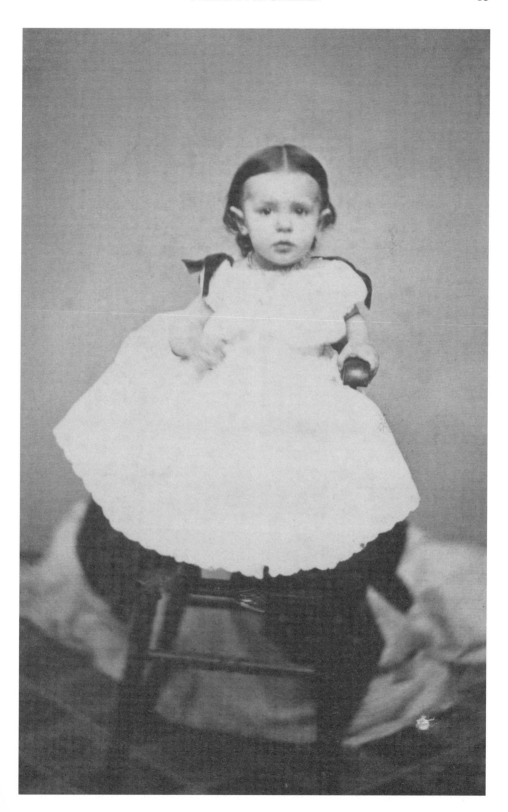

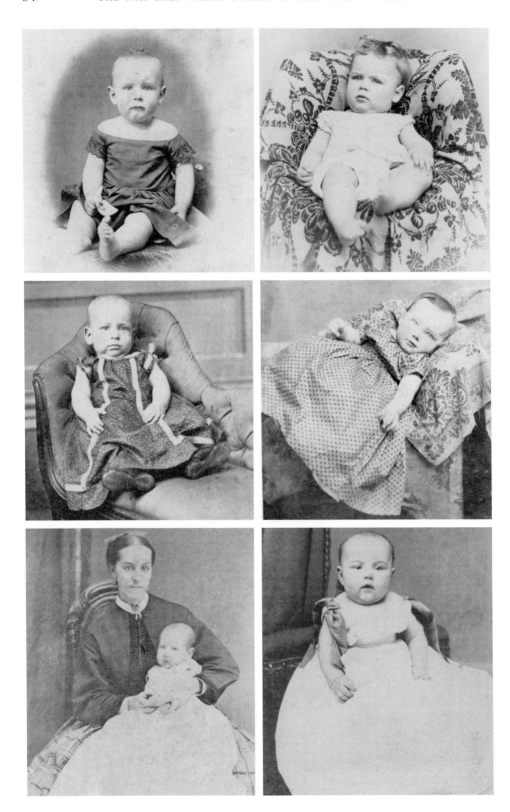

Girls

TODDLERS • YOUNG GIRLS • ADOLESCENTS • TEENAGERS

The majority of girls had hairstyles that were parted in the middle with no bangs and short, blunt cut sides and back. Hats rather than bonnets were most often worn as head covers. Necklaces were common and were at times worn as "protection" against illness. The one piece boat necked, gathered bodice, buttoned in the back dress with short sleeves and full skirt was the typical attire for young girls. The dress design changed to a higher neckline, longer sleeves and hem length as the girl matured. Leather shoes for girls were either slip-on with an ankle strap or front or side laced boots.

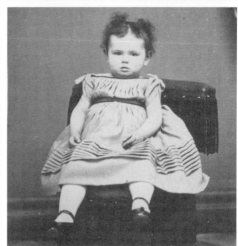

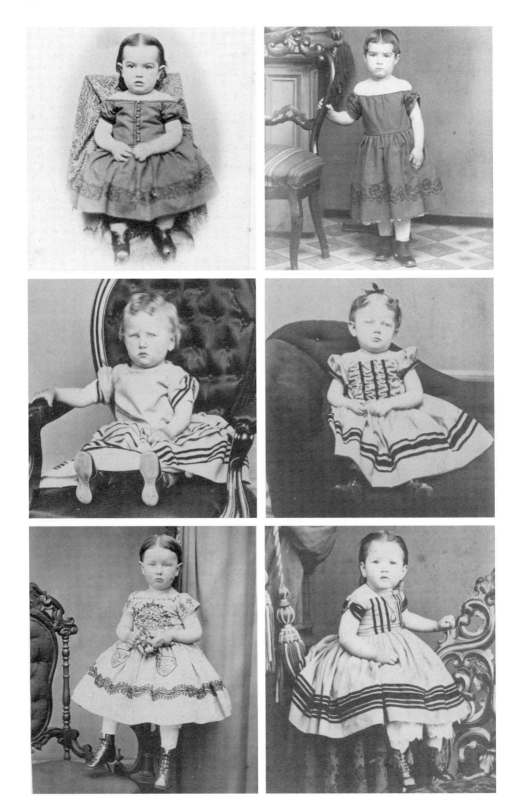

The Garibaldi blouse and skirt with the Zouave jacket was a new fashion that the older girls fancied.

Boys

Boys' hair was kept short and parted on the side of the head. They wore dresses until they were potty trained and sometimes longer. Then they graduated to wearing shirts that buttoned onto the waistband of knee length pants or long trousers. As they grew older, their styles of clothing became more like the adult males, wearing hats and jackets in addition to the long trousers and cotton shirts.

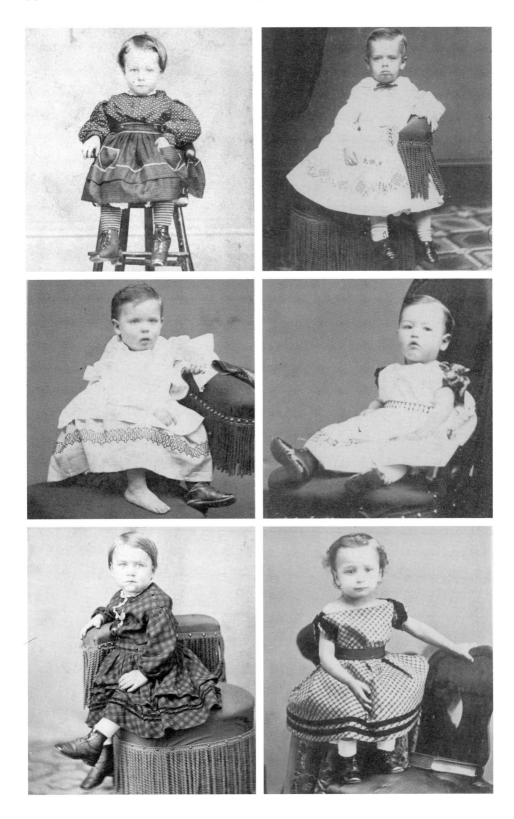

3
Fashions for Men

HAIR AND HATS • NECK WEAR AND VESTS • COATS AND TROUSERS

Hair and Hats

Hairstyles for most men were the basic short cut with a part on the side of the head. Beards and chin hair were as common as a clean-shaven face, but mustaches alone were seen less often.

The hat was considered part of a man's proper attire. Therefore, hats of all shapes and styles were worn. They were made of straw, wool or fur felt. Hat brim width varied along with crown height.

Neck Wear & Vests

Neck wear was always worn in public by men of all ages. There were several different styles of bow ties, cravats and ascots. Size of the neck wear varied from small to very large and flamboyant. Solid, stripped or patterned silk or fine cotton were the fabric of choice for neck wear.

Men's vests were most often collared and single breasted. They were made from colorful solid or printed silk, wool, or cotton fabrics. The vest was the most elaborate part of the man's attire which often included very fancy buttons. A pocket watch chain was frequently attached to the vest button and the watch was tucked into the vest pocket.

Coats & Trousers

The man's coat was considered an essential garment since it had to be worn to cover his shirt while he was in public. It was mainly made of a solid color wool with a single or double breasted front. Coat pocket placement and button types varied. The hem length of the coat fell either at the top of the thigh or at the knee. The shorter length coat was considered less formal than the longer coat.

Durable wool, cotton or linen was the most common fabric used for men's trousers. Although solid colors trousers were prevalent, tweeds, stripes and plaids were considered trendy. The trouser fabric and color did not always match the coat. The legs of the trousers were wide and straight without cuffs.

4
Family and Friends

Husbands & Wives • Sisters • Brothers

Photos with two or more people are especially interesting because of the comparison that can be made amongst the subjects in the photo. Different styles of clothing and hair, fabric and accessory usage and economic status are evident.

If you enjoyed this book, you will also like the first volume of

The Way They Were: Dressed in 1860-1865.

Published in 2008, Donna Abraham's first book has 160 pages of full-frame CDVs from her private collection and is a superb photographic reference of civilian clothing. Every image in these two books reveals a multitude of details and they are a "must have" for every costume designer and living historian.

Additional Reading

Arnold, Janet, *Patterns of Fashion 1*, New York: Drama Book Publishers, 1983.

Arnold, Janet, *Patterns of Fashion 2*, New York: Drama Book Publishers, 1993.

Atkins, Bernadette Loeffel, *Widow's Weeds And Weeping Veils*, Gettysburg: B. L. Atkins, 2004.

Bell, C. Jeannenne, *Collector's Encyclopedia Of Hairwirk Jewelry*, Paducah: Collector Books, 1998.

Bell, Jeanenne, *Answers To Questions About Old Jewelry "1850 To 1950,"* Florance: Books Americana, 1992.

Bradfield, Nancy, *Costume In Detail 1730-1930*, New York: Costume and Fashion Press, 2003.

Brown III, William L., *Thoughts On Men's Shirts In America 1750-1900*, Gettysburg: Thomas Publications, 1999.

Bruton, LaRee Johnson, *Ladies' Vintage Accessories Identification and Value Guide*, Paducah: Collectors' Books, 2001.

Cross, Mary Bywater, *Quilts of the Oregon Trail*, Atglen: Schiffer, 2007.

Fales, Martha Gandy, *Jewelry in America 1600-1900*, Woodbridge: Antique Collector's Club Ltd., 1995.

Gadsby, Chet, *Victorian Paisley Shawls*, Atglen: Schiffer, 2002.

Kaplan, Authur Guy, *Official Identification and Price Guide to Antique Jewelry*, New York: The House of Collectables, 1990.

Langley, Susan, *Vintage Hats and Bonnets1790-1970*, Paducah: Collector Books, 1998.

Leisch, Juanita, *An Introduction To Civil War Civilians*, Gettysburg: Thomas Publications, 1994.

Leisch, Juanita, *Who Wore What?*, Gettysburg: Thomas Publications, 1995.

Mace, O. Henry, *Collector's Guide To Early Photographs*, Lola: Krause Publications, 1999.

Meller, Susan and Elffers, Joost, *Textile Designs*, New York: Harry N. Abrams, 1991.

Osborne, Peggy Ann, *About Buttons A Collector's Guide*, Atglen: Schiffer, 1994.

Severa, Joan, *Dressed For The Photographer*, Kent: The Kent State University Press, 1995.

Toomer, Heather, *Antique Lace Identifying Types and Techniques*, Aglen: Schiffer, 2001.

Trestain, Eileen Jahnke, *Dating Fabrics A Color Guide 1800-1960*, Paducah: American Quilter's Society, 1998.

About the Author

Donna Abraham is a retired teacher and the founder of Abraham's Lady, LLC. She is in charge of all product development, purchasing, and sales for the business. Her first book, *The Way They Were: Dressed In 1860-1865,* was published in 2008. *Volume 2* is a compilation of the remainder of her photo collection.

Donna lives in Gettysburg, PA and spends her free time playing with her four grandchildren, reading, collecting antiques, and vacationing with her husband in Florida.